MW01061627

for the Sunday Lectionary

BY SUSAN E. MYERS

LITURGY
TRAINING
PUBLICATIONS

ACKNOWLEDGMENTS

This book was edited by Martin Connell. Audrey Novak
Riley and Bryan Cones were the production editors. The
design is by Anna Manhart, and the typesetting was done
by Karen Mitchell in Goudy. Printed by Bawden Printing
in Eldridge, Iowa. The cover art is by Barbara Simcoe.

ISBN 1-56854-297-6

PRONUN

INTRODUCTION

This pronunciation guide is intended especially
for readers at liturgy on Sundays and feast days.
The ministry of proclaiming the word of God in an
assembly gathered for prayer is a ministry that is
demanding, enlightening and inspiring. Although
it requires certain skills and knowledge, the very
task of preparing and proclaiming liturgical readings
forms a person and helps to make you worthy of the
awesome responsibility entrusted to you. If you are
open to the movement of the Spirit of God in your
heart, you will be able to communicate that to
your listeners. This guide will provide some practical
tips as well.

Proclaiming the readings during the liturgy
of the word at Sunday Mass or on feast days is far
more than merely providing an introduction to the
liturgy of the eucharist or giving a history lesson
or telling an entertaining story. When we read from
or hear the scriptures, we become part of an ongoing
story. We share in the journey of a people attempt-
ing to understand God and their relationship with
the divine; we identify with their joys and sorrows,
their struggles and victories. Whether we are reading
about the attempts of the Hebrew people to be
true to God's expectations of them or the excite-
ment of the early Christians enlivened by the belief
that God has acted decisively in the person of Jesus,
we can see that the particular events and attitudes
of this people, though unique and specific to them,
also have far-reaching implications. We struggle
with the same temptations they do, we make many
of the same mistakes, we misunderstand and lose
our way. We also sing and dance and rejoice in the
many blessings we see around us, confident that
we are being called to an ever-fuller life and closer
union with God.

As the minister of the word of God, you have not only the task of assisting your congregation in understanding the readings, but also the responsibility of teaching and challenging, comforting and encouraging. You do this by the way you proclaim each reading, by your phrasing and your enunciation, by your voice and your posture. The more you understand and take to heart the message you offer your listeners, and the better prepared you are to share it with them, the more successful will be your ministry as you allow God to act through you.

Your vocation of proclaiming God's word begins in private or in a small group as you read and meditate upon the selection you will share with your community. You may wish to read it in its biblical context in order to see what precedes and follows the verses you will read. You can find more on the history and meaning of your passage in a commentary or workbook designed for the purpose. Then try to become part of the story or imagine yourself as a recipient of the message given. Don't worry if the passage is not entirely clear or if the practices or attitudes seem foreign to you. What is important is that you are willing to learn, like the first recipients of the text, what God is communicating through it. Reflect on it; pray about it.

Then practice the reading. Be certain that you know how to pronounce every word. Plan your phrasing and know when you will pause, when you will raise your voice and when you will speak softly. Read it aloud several times until you are comfortable that you are ready.

When it is time for you to read, take a deep breath. Move and speak slowly and clearly, enunciating every word. It may seem as though you are reading too slowly or are adding too much emphasis and inflection, but it probably appears quite different to your listeners. In whatever you do, remain confident. If you stumble over a term or forget the pronunciation of a word, simply read as clearly as you can, then continue as you have prepared.

To draw attention to an error gives your listeners the mistaken impression that this is your performance. Rather, you are the vessel through whom God is communicating with this people. To present the divine word effectively, you must have faith in your abilities and, at the same time, be willing to step back and allow God to work through you. Be humble, yet confident. You have been chosen.

This guide focuses on words and phrases that may be unfamiliar or easily confused with other words. It is not meant to be exhaustive, but contains only terms from the lectionary readings.

Alternative pronunciations are sometimes provided, since there may be several legitimate ways to render a name from the original Aramaic, Hebrew or Greek into English. This guide attempts to offer pronunciations that make sense in English, while remaining true to the original language as much as possible. Choose a pronunciation that sounds right to you and memorize it.

I have attempted to find the simplest means possible to indicate the pronunciations of terms in this guide. Most consonants in English are straightforward: The letter B always represents the sound B and D is always D, and so on. Vowels are more complicated. Note that the long I sound (as in kite or ice) is represented by i̅, while long A (skate, pray) is represented by ay. Long E (beam, marine) is represented by ee; long O (boat, coat) by oh; long U (sure, secure) is represented by oo or yoo. Short A (cat), E (bed), I (slim) and O (dot) are represented by a, e, i and o except in an unstressed syllable, when E and I are signified by eh and ih. Short U (cup) is represented by uh. An asterisk (*) indicates the schwa sound, as in the last syllable of the word "stable". The letters OO and TH can each be pronounced in two ways (as in cool or book; thin or they); underlining differentiates between them. Stress is indicated by the capitalization of the stressed syllable in words of more than one syllable. Please consult the key for more details.

PRONUNCIATION KEY

Capitalization indicates stressed syllable(s).

bait = bayt
cat = kat
sang = sang
father = FAH-<u>th</u>er
care = kayr
paw = paw
jar = jahr

easy = EE-zee
her = her
let = let
queen = kween
delude = deh-L<u>OO</u>D
when = hwen

ice = īs
if = if
finesse = fih-NES
thin = thin
vision = VIZH-*n
ship = ship
sir = ser

gloat = gloht
cot = kot
noise = noyz
poison = POY-z*n
plow = plow
although = awl-<u>TH</u>OH

church = church
fun = fuhn
fur = fer
flute = fl<u>oo</u>t
foot = foot

Aaron	AYR-uhn
Abba	AH-bah
Abel	AY-b*l
Abel-meholah	AY-b*l muh-HOH-lah
Abiathar	uh-BĪ-uh-thahr
Abijah	uh-BĪ-juh
Abilene	ab-uh-LEEN; ab-uh-LEE-nee
Abishai	uh-BĪSH-ay-ī; uh-BĪ-shī
Abiud	uh-BĪ-uhd
Abner	AB-ner
Abraham	AY-bruh-ham
Abram	AY-br*m
absurdity	ab-SOOR-dih-tee; uhb-SOOR-dih-tee; ab-ZOOR-dih-tee; uhb-ZOOR-dih-tee
abyss	uh-BIS
accompaniment	uh-KUHM-p*-nee- m*nt
accordance	uh-KOHRD-*ns
accursed	uh-KERST; uh-KER-sid
accusation	ak-yoo-ZAY-shuhn
Achaia	uh-KEE-uh; uh-KAY-yuh
Achim	AH-kim; AY-kim
Achor	AY-kohr

acquittal	uh-KWIT-*l
Acts	akts
Adam	AD-*m
adherence	ad-HEER-*ns
Admah	AD-mah
administer	ad-MIN-ih-ster
administrator	ad-MIN-ih-stray-ter
admonish	ad-MON-ish
adultery	uh-DUHL-ter-ee
adversary	AD-ver-sayr-ee
adversity	ad-VER-sih-tee
Advocate (noun)	AD-voh-k*t
Ahaz	AY-haz
alabaster	AL-uh-bas-ter
Alexander	al-ig-ZAN-der
allege	uh-LEJ
alleluia	ah-lay-LOO-yuh
allot	uh-LOT
allure	uh-LOOR
alms	olmz; ahmz
aloes	AL-ohz
Alpha	AHL-fuh; AL-fuh
Alphaeus	AL-fee-uhs
Amalek	AM-uh-lek
Amaziah	am-uh-ZĪ-uh
ambassador	am-BAS-uh-der; am-BAS-uh-dohr

amen	ah-MEN; ay-MEN
Aminadab	uh-MIN-uh-dab
Amminadab	uh-MIN-uh-dab
Ammonites	AM-uh-nīts
Amorites	AM-er-īts
Amos	AY-m*s
Amoz	AY-muhz
Andrew	AN-dr<u>oo</u>
Anna	AN-uh
Annas	AN-uhs
antimony	AN-tih-moh-nee
Antioch	AN-tee-ahk
anxiety	ang-ZĪ-eh-tee
anxious	ANGK-shuhs; ANG-shuhs
Apollos	uh-POL-ohs
Apostles	uh-POS-*lz
apportion	uh-POHR-shuhn
Arabah	AYR-uh-buh
Arabia	uh-RAY-bee-uh
Arabs	AYR-uhbz
Aram	AYR-uhm
Aramean	ayr-uh-MEE-uhn
arbitrate	AHR-bih-trayt
arbitrator	AHR-bih-tray-ter
Archelaus	ahr-kih-LAY-uhs
Arimathea	ayr-ih-muh-THEE-uh

aromatic	ayr-oh-MAT-ik
arrogance	AYR-uh-g*ns
arrogant	AYR-uh-g*nt
Asa	AY-suh; AH-sah
Asaph	AY-saf
Asher	ASH-er
Asia	AY-zhuh
assurance	uh-SHOOR-*ns
assuredly	uh-SHOOR-uhd-lee
Assyria	uh-SEER-ee-uh
astrologers	uh-STRAHL-uh-jerz
atonement	uh-TOHN-m*nt
Attalia	uh-TAHL-ee-uh; at-uh-LĪ-uh
Augustus	aw-GUHS-tuhs
avarice	AV-uh-ris
Azor	AY-zohr
Baal	BAH-ahl; BAY-uhl
Baal-shalishah	BAH-ahl shahl-ih-SHAH; BAY-uhl shahl-ih-SHAH
Babel	BAB-*l; BAY-b*l
Babylon	BAB-ih-lon
Baptist	BAP-tist
Baptizer	bap-TĪ-zer

Barabbas	buh-RAB-uhs
barbarian	bahr-BAYR-ee-uhn
Barnabas	BAHR-nuh-buhs
barricade	BAYR-ih-kayd
Barsabbas	bahr-SAH-buhs; bahr-SAB-uhs
Bartholomew	bahr-THAHL- uh-my<u>oo</u>
Bartimaeus	bahr-tih-MAY-uhs; bahr-tih-MEE-uhs
Baruch	buh-R<u>OO</u>K
Beelzebul	bee-EL-zeh-buhl
benefactor	BEN-eh-fak-ter
Benjamin	BEN-juh-muhn
bereft	beh-REFT
bestow	bih-STOH
Bethany	BETH-uh-nee
Bethel	BETH-*l
Bethlehem	BETH-luh-hem
Bethphage	BETH-fayj; BETH-fuh-jee
Bethsaida	beth-SAY-ih-duh
bier	beer
bitumen	bih-T<u>OO</u>-m*n; bih-TYOO-m*n
blaspheme	blas-FEEM
blasphemy	BLAS-fuh-mee
Boaz	BOH-az

bosom	BOOZ-uhm; B<u>OO</u>Z-uhm
bow (rainbow)	boh
bow (verb)	bow
brazier	BRAY-zher
briers	BRĪ-erz
brigand	BRIG-*nd
brow	brow
buffets	BUF-its
burial	BAYR-ee-uhl
bury	BAYR-ee
Caesar	SEE-zer
Caesarea	sez-uh-REE-uh; see-zuh-REE-uh
Caiaphas	KĪ-uh-fuhs; KAY-uh-fuhs
calamity	kuh-LAM-ih-tee
Cana	KAY-nuh
Canaan	KAY-n*n
Canaanite	KAY-nuh-nīt
Capernaum	kuh-PER-nee-*m; kuh-PER-nay-*m; kuh-PER-n*m
Cappadocia	kap-uh-DOH-shuh; kap-uh-DOH-shee-uh
captivate	KAP-tih-vayt
caravan	KAYR-uh-van
carbuncles	KAHR-bung-k*lz
carcass	KAHR-kuhs

Carmel	KAHR-m*l
carnal	KAHR-n*l
carnelian	kahr-NEEL-yuhn
carousing	kuh-ROW-zing
celebration	sel-uh-BRAY-shuhn
cenacle	SEN-uh-k*l
centurion	sen-TOOR-ee-uhn; sen-TYOOR-ee-uhn
Cephas	SEE-fuhs
ceremonial	ser-uh-MOH-nee-uhl
Chaldeans	kal-DEE-uhnz; kahl-DEE-uhnz
charioteer	chayr-ee-uh-TEER
chasm	KAZ-*m
chastise	chas-TĪZ
Chloe	KLOH-ee
Christ	krīst
Christian	KRIS-chuhn
Chronicles	KRAH-nih-k*ls
Chuza	KOO-zuh; KYOO-zuh
Cilicia	sih-LISH-uh; sih-LISH-ee-uh
circumcise	SER-kuhm-sīz
circumcision	ser-kuhm-SIH-zhuhn
cistern	SIS-tern
clamorous	KLAM-er-uhs
cleansed	klenzd

clemency	KLEM-*n-see
Cleopas	KLEE-oh-puhs
Clopas	KLOH-puhs
cloth (noun)	klawth
clothe (verb)	kloh<u>th</u>
cohort	KOH-hohrt
Colossians	kuh-LOSH-uhnz
comfortable	KUHM-fer-tuh-b*l
commend	kuh-MEND
commendation	kah-men-DAY-shuhn
communal	kuh-MYOON-*l; KOM-yoo-n*l
compassionate	kuhm-PASH-uhn-uht
compel	kuhm-PEL
competent	KOM-puh-t*nt
complacent	kuhm-PLAY-s*nt
conceit	kuhn-SEET
conceive	kuhn-SEEV
condemn	kuhn-DEM
condemnation	kon-d*m-NAY-shuhn
confer	kuhn-FER
conscience	KON-shuhns
consecrate	KON-suh-krayt
consequently	KON-suh-kwent-lee
consolation	kon-suh-LAY-shuhn
console	kuhn-SOHL
constancy	KON-stuhn-see

contemplate	KON-tuhm-playt
contemptible	kuhn-TEMP-tuh-b*l
contention	k*n-TEN-shuhn
contrary	KON-tray-ree
contributor	kuhn-TRIB-yoo-ter
controversy	KON-truh-ver-see
Corinthians	kohr-IN-thee-uhnz
Cornelius	kohr-NEEL-yuhs
corruptible	kohr-RUPT-uh-b*l
countenance	KOWN-tuh-n*ns
courageous	ker-RAY-juhs
covenant	KUHV-eh-n*nt
covet	KUHV-it
cowardice	KOW-er-dis
cowardly	KOW-erd-lee
Cretans	KREE-tuhns
crucifixion	kroo-sih-FIK-shuhn
crucify	KROO-sih-fī
cultivation	kuhl-tih-VAY-shuhn
curds	kerds
Cushite	KOOSH-īt
cymbal	SIM-buhl
Cyrene	sī-REE-nee
Cyrenian	sī-REE-nee-uhn
Cyrus	SĪ-ruhs
Damascus	duh-MAS-kuhs
dandle	DAN-d*l

Daniel	DAN-yuhl
David	DAY-vid
debauchery	dih-BAW-chuh-ree
debt	det
debtor	DET-er
Decapolis	dih-KAP-uh-lis
deceit	dih-SEET
decrepit	dih-KREP-it
defense	dih-FENS
deference	DEF-uh-rens
defraud	dih-FRAWD
deity	DEE-ih-tee
delegation	del-eh-GAY-shuhn
deliberations	dih-lib-uh-RAY-shuhnz
demoralize	dih-MOHR-uhl-īz
denarius	dih-NAHR-ee-uhs
denarii	dih-NAHR-ee-ī
departure	dih-PAR-cher
Derbe	DER-bee
descendant	dih-SEN-d*nt
desert (noun)	DEZ-ert
desert (verb)	dih-ZERT
desolate	DES-uh-lit
despise	dih-SPĪZ
despondent	dih-SPAHN-d*nt
destine	DES-tin

detest	dih-TEST
Deuteronomy	d<u>oo</u>-ter-AH-nuh-mee; dy<u>oo</u>-ter-AH-nuh-mee
devious	DEE-vee-uhs
devour	dih-VOWR
diadem	DI-uh-dem
dictate (noun)	DIK-tayt
dignitary	DIG-nih-tay-ree
diligent	DIL-ih-j*nt
discern	dih-SERN
discernment	dih-SERN-m*nt
disciple	dih-SĪ-p*l
discipline	DIS-ih-plin
discord	DIS-kohrd
disdain	dis-DAYN
disembark	dis-em-BAHRK
disheveled	dih-SHEV-uhld
dislocate	DIS-loh-kayt; dis-LOH-kayt
dismal	DIZ-muhl
disorder	dis-OHR-der
dispense	dis-PENS
dissension	dih-SEN-shuhn
dissipation	dis-ih-PAY-shuhn
dissolute	DIS-uh-l<u>oo</u>t
dissolution	dis-uh-L<u>OO</u>-shuhn
dissuade	dih-SWAYD
distinguished	dis-TING-gwishd

distress	dis-TRES
division	dih-VIZH-uhn
docile	DOS-*l
domination	dom-ih-NAY-shuhn
dominion	doh-MIN-yuhn
dromedary	DROM-eh-dayr-ee
drought	drowt
dungeon	DUHN-juhn
Ebed-melech	EH-bid-MEH-lik
Ecclesiastes	ih-klee-zee-AS-teez
ecstasy	EK-stuh-see
Eden	EE-d*n
Edom	EE-d*m
Egypt	EE-jipt
Egyptians	ee-JIP-shuhnz
Elamites	EE-luh-mīts
Eldad	EL-dad
Eleazar	el-ee-AY-zer
elemental	el-uh-MEN-tuhl
Eli	EE-lī
Eli, Eli, lema sabachthani	ay-LEE, ay-LEE, luh-MAH sah-bahk-TAH-nee
Eliab	ee-LĪ-uhb
Eliakim	ee-LĪ-uh-kim
Eliezer	el-ee-AY-zer
Elijah	ee-LĪ-juh

Elisha	ee-LĪ-shuh
Eliud	ee-LĪ-uhd
Elizabeth	ee-LIZ-uh-beth
Elkanah	el-KAY-nah
Eloi, Eloi, lama sabachthani	el-oh-EE, el-oh-EE, LAH-muh sah-bahk-TAH-nee; ay-loh-EE . . .
Eloi, Eloi, lema sabachthani	el-oh-EE, el-oh-EE, luh-MAH sah-bahk-TAH-nee; ay-loh-EE . . .
eloquence	EL-uh-kwens
elusive	ih-LOO-siv
ember	EM-ber
Emmanuel	ee-MAN-yoo-el
Emmaus	eh-MAY-uhs
encumbrance	en-KUHM-br*ns
endurance	en-DOOR-*ns; en-DYOOR-*ns
enjoin	en-JOYN
enmity	EN-mih-tee
entail	en-TAYL
envelop (verb)	en-VEL-uhp
envious	EN-vee-uhs
ephah	EE-fah
Ephesians	ee-FEE-zhuhnz
Ephesus	EF-uh-suhs

ephphatha	EF-fah-thah
Ephraim	EE-fray-im; EF-r*m
Ephrathah	EF-ruh-thuh
equity	EK-wih-tee
espouse	es-POWS
Ethiopian	ee-thee-OH-pee-uhn
Euphrates	yoo-FRAY-teez
ewe	yoo
Excellency	EK-sel-len-see
exception	ek-SEP-shuhn
exhaustion	eg-ZAWS-chuhn
exhort	eg-ZOHRT
exhortation	eg-zohr-TAY-shuhn
Exile	EG-zīl; EK-sīl
Exodus	EK-suh-duhs
expiate	EK-spee-ayt
expiation	ek-spee-AY-shuhn
extinguish	ek-STING-gwish
extort	ek-STOHRT
extortion	ek-STOHR-shuhn
extraordinary	ek-STROHR-duh-nayr-ee
exult	eg-ZULHT
Ezekiel	ee-ZEE-kee-uhl
Ezra	EZ-ruh
facade	fuh-SAHD

famine	FAM-in
famished	FAM-isht
Father	FAH-<u>th</u>er
festal	FES-tuhl
fidelity	fih-DEL-uh-tee; fī-DEL-uh-tee
fiend	feend
figuratively	FIG-yer-uh-tiv-lee
firmament	FER-muh-m*nt
flog	flog; flawg
fodder	FOD-er
forbade	fohr-BAD; fohr-BAYD
forbearance	fohr-BAYR-*ns
foreign	FOHR-uhn
foreknowledge	FOHR-nahl-ij
forfeit	FOHR-fuht
fornication	fohr-nih-KAY-shuhn
fragmentary	FRAG-m*n-tayr-ee
frankincense	FRANGK-in-sens
fugitive	FY<u>OO</u>-jih-tiv
fuller's lye	FUHL-ers lī
fullers' soap	FUHL-ers sohp
futile	FY<u>OO</u>-t*l
Gabbatha	GAB-uh-thuh
Gabriel	GAY-bree-uhl
Galatia	guh-LAY-shuh; guh-LAY-shee-uh

Galatians	guh-LAY-shuhnz
Galilean	gal-ih-LEE-uhn
Galilee	GAL-ih-lee
gall	gawl
Gedaliah	ged-uh-LĪ-uh
Gehazi	geh-HAY-zī
Gehenna	geh-HEN-nah
genealogy	jee-nee-AL-uh-jee; jee-nee-OL-uh-jee
generative	JEN-er-uh-tiv
Genesis	JEN-uh-sis
Gennesaret	geh-NES-uh-ret
Gentiles	JEN-tīls
genuflect	JEN-yoo-flekt
genuineness	JEN-yoo-in-nes
Gethsemane	geth-SEM-uh-nee
Gethsemani	geth-SEM-uh-nee
Gibeon	GIB-ee-uhn
Gilgal	GIL-gahl
gird	gerd
glorify	GLOHR-ih-fī
gnash	nash
Golgotha	GOL-guh-thuh; GAWL-guh-thuh
Gomorrah	guh-MOHR-ah
gong	gawng
gorges	GOHR-juhz
gouge	gowj

granary	GRAYN-uh-ree
Greek	greek
grievances	GREE-v*n-suhz
Habakkuk	huh-BAK-kuhk; HAB-uh-kuhk
Hadadrimmon	hay-dad-RIM-uhn
Hades	HAY-deez
hallelujah	hah-lay-L$\underline{OO}$-yuh
hallowed	HAL-ohd
Hannah	HAN-uh
hasten	HAY-suhn
Haran	HAYR-uhn
hearth	hahrth
Hebrews	HEE-br$\underline{oo}$z
Hebron	HEB-ruhn
heifer	HEF-er
heir	ayr
Hellenist	HEL-uh-nist
hemorrhage	HEM-er-rij
henceforth	HENS-fohrth
heritage	HAYR-ih-tij
Herod	HAYR-uhd
Herodian	her-OH-dee-uhn
Hezekiah	hez-eh-KĪ-uh
Hezron	HEZ-ruhn
Hilkia	hil-KĪ-uh
hireling	HĪR-ling

Hittite	HIT-tīt
Hivite	HIH-vīt
hoarfrost	HOHR-frawst
hoist	hoyst
holocaust	HOL-uh-kawst;
	HOH-luh-kawst
Holy Spirit	HOH-lee SPEER-it
homage	OM-ij;
	HOM-ij
honor	ON-er
Horeb	HOHR-eb
Hosanna	hoh-ZAH-nah
Hosannah	hoh-ZAH-nah
Hosea	hoh-ZAY-uh
hostile	HOS-t*l
hostility	hos-TIL-uh-tee
humiliation	hy<u>oo</u>-mil-ee-AY-shuhn
humility	hyoo-MIL-ih-tee
Hur	her
hypocrite	HIP-uh-krit
hyssop	HIS-uhp
Iconium	ī-KOH-nee-uhm
idolatry	ī-DOL-uh-tree
illicit	ih-LIS-it
Immanuel	im-MAN-y<u>oo</u>-el
immerse	ih-MERS
immorality	im-oh-RAL-ih-tee
immortal	ih-MOHR-t*l

immortality	im-ohr-TAL-ih-tee
immovable	ih-MOO-vuh-b*l
impediment	im-PED-uh-m*nt
imperishability	im-payr-ih-shuh-BIL-ih-tee
imperishable	im-PAYR-ih-shuh-b*l
impiety	im-PĪ-eh-tee
impious	IM-pee-uhs
imprisonment	im-PRIZ-uhn-m*nt
improvise	IM-pruh-vīz
impudence	IM-pyoo-d*ns
impudent	IM-pyoo-d*nt
inapproachable	in-uh-PROH-chuh-b*l
incite	in-SĪT
incorruptibility	in-koh-ruhp-tuh-BIL-ih-tee
incorruptible	in-koh-RUHP-tuh-b*l
incorruption	in-koh-RUHP-shuhn
incredulous	in-KRED-yoo-luhs; in-KREJ-uh-luhs
indescribable	in-dih-SKRĪ-buh-b*l
indulgence	in-DUHL-j*ns
industrious	in-DUHS-tree-uhs
infirmity	in-FER-mih-tee
infuriate	in-FYOOR-ee-ayt
inhabited	in-HAB-ih-tuhd
inheritance	in-HER-ih-t*ns
iniquity	ih-NIK-wih-tee

initiative	ih-NISH-ee-uh-tiv; ih-NISH-uh-tiv
innumerable	ih-N<u>OO</u>-mer-uh-b*l; ih-NY<u>OO</u>-mer-uh-b*l
inscrutable	in-SKR<u>OO</u>-tuh-b*l
insistent	in-SIS-t*nt
insolence	IN-suh-l*ns
insurgents	in-SER-j*nts
insurrection	in-suh-REK-shuhn
integrity	in-TEG-rih-tee
intercede	in-ter-SEED
intercession	in-ter-SESH-uhn
interrogate	in-TAYR-uh-gayt
interrogation	in-tayr-uh-GAY-shuhn
intervene	in-ter-VEEN
intoxicants	in-TOK-sih-k*nts
irreproachable	eer-rih-PROH-chuh-b*l
irritable	EER-ih-tuh-b*l
Isaac	Ī-zik
Isaiah	ī-ZAY-uh
Iscariot	is-KAYR-ee-uht
Israel	IZ-ree-uhl; IZ-ray-uhl
Israelite	IZ-ree-uh-līt; IZ-ray-uh-līt
Ituraea	ih-t<u>oo</u>-REE-ah
jackal	JAK-uhl
Jacob	JAY-kuhb

Jairus	jay-Ī-ruhs; JĪ-ruhs
James	jaymz
jasper	JAS-per
Javan	JAY-vuhn
Jebusites	JEB-yoo-sīts
Jechoniah	jek-oh-NĪ-uh
Jehoshaphat	jeh-HOH-shuh-fat
Jehu	JAY-hoo
Jeremiah	jayr-uh-MĪ-uh
Jericho	JAYR-ih-koh
Jerusalem	juh-ROO-suh-lem; juh-ROO-zuh-lem
Jesse	JES-ee
Jesus	JEE-zuhz; JEE-zuhs
Jesus'	JEE-zuhz; JEE-zuhs (not JEE-zuh-zuhz)
Jethro	JETH-roh
Joanna	joh-AN-uh
Job	johb
Joel	JOH-*l
John	jon
Jonah	JOH-nuh
Joram	JOHR-uhm
Jordan	JOHR-d*n
Joseph	JOH-sif; JOH-zuhf

Joses	JOH-seez; JOH-sez
Joshua	JOSH-<u>oo</u>-uh; JOSH-y<u>oo</u>-uh
Josiah	joh-SĪ-uh
Jotham	JOH-thuhm
jubilation	j<u>oo</u>-bih-LAY-shuhn
Jucal	J<u>OO</u>-kuhl
Judah	J<u>OO</u>-duh
Judaism	J<u>OO</u>-duh-iz-*m; J<u>OO</u>-dee-iz-*m
Judas	J<u>OO</u>-duhs
Judea	j<u>oo</u>-DEE-uh; j<u>oo</u>-DAY-uh
jurisdiction	jer-uhs-DIK-shuhn
justification	juhs-tuh-fih-KAY-shun
Justus	JUS-tuhs
Kephas	KEE-fuhs
Kidron	KID-ruhn
kiln	kiln; kil
kilometer	kih-LOM-uh-ter
kilometre	kih-LOM-uh-ter
Kings	kingz
knead	need
lair	layr
Lamentations	lam-en-TAY-shuhnz
Laodicea	lay-ahd-ih-SEE-uh
lava	LAH-vuh

lavish	LAV-ish
Lazarus	LAZ-uh-ruhs
leavened	LEV-uhnd
Lebanon	LEB-uh-nuhn
legion	LEE-juhn
leper	LEP-er
leprosy	LEP-ruh-see
leprous	LEP-ruhs
Levi	LEE-vī
Levite	LEE-vīt
Leviticus	lih-VIT-ih-kuhs
liable	LĪ-uh-b*l
libations	lī-BAY-shuhnz
Libya	LIB-ee-uh
licentious	lī-SEN-shuhs
lineage	LIN-ee-ij
lintel	LIN-t*l
loathe	LOH<u>TH</u>
loincloths	LOYN-klaw<u>th</u>z; LOYN-klawths
loins	loynz
Lord	lohrd
Lot	lot
Lud	luhd
Luke	l<u>oo</u>k
luminaries	L<u>OO</u>-mih-nayr-eez

luxuriously	luhg-ZHOOR-ee-uhs-lee; luhk-SHOOR-ee-uhs-lee
lyre	līr
Lysanias	li-SAY-nee-uhs
Lystra	LĪS-truh
Maccabees	MAK-uh-beez
Macedonia	mas-eh-DOH-nee-uh
Magdalene	MAG-duh-luhn; MAG-duh-leen; MAG-duh-lehn
Malachi	MAL-uh-kī
Malchiah	mal-KĪ-uh
Malchus	MAL-kuhs
malefactor	MAL-uh-fak-ter
malice	MAL-is
malicious	muh-LISH-uhs
maltreat	mal-TREET
mammon	MAM-uhn
Mamre	MAHM-ray; MAM-ree
Manasseh	muh-NAS-uh
manifestation	man-ih-fes-TAY-shuhn
manna	MAN-uh
manure	muh-NOOR; muh-NYOOR
marauder	muh-RAW-der
Mark	mahrk

marrow	MAYR-oh
Martha	MAHR-thah
Mary	MAYR-ee
Massah	MAS-ah; MAH-sah
Mattan	MAT-uhn
Matthan	MATH-uhn
Matthew	MATH-yoo
Matthias	muh-THĪ-uhs
mature	muh-TYOOR; muh-TOOR; muh-CHOOR
Medad	MEE-dad
Medes	meedz
mediator	MEE-dee-ay-ter
Megiddo	meh-GID-doh
Melchizedek	mel-KIZ-ih-dek; mel-KEEZ-ih-dek
menstruous	MEN-stroo-uhs
merciful	MER-sih-fuhl
Meribah	MAYR-ih-bah
Mesopotamia	mes-uh-poh-TAY-mee-uh
Messiah	meh-SĪ-uh
Micah	MĪ-kuh
Michael	MĪ-k*l
Midian	MID-ee-uhn
miraculous	mih-RAK-yoo-luhs
mirage	mih-RAHZH

mire	mīr
Miriam	MEER-ee-uhm
mitre	MĪ-ter
molten	MOHL-t*n
moor	m<u>oo</u>r
Moriah	moh-RĪ-uh
mosaic	moh-ZAY-ik
Moses	MOH-ziz; MOH-zis
Moses'	MOH-ziz; MOH-zis (not MOH-ziz-ziz)
Mosoch	MOH-sok
Mount	mownt
mulberry	MUL-bayr-ee; MUL-buh-ree
multitude	MUL-tih-t<u>oo</u>d
myriad	MEER-ee-uhd
myrrh	mer
Naaman	NAY-uh-muhn
Nahshon	NAH-shuhn
Naim	naym
Nain	nayn
Naphtali	NAF-tuh-lee
nard	nahrd
Nathan	NAY-thuhn
Nathanael	nuh-THAN-ee-uhl
Nazarene	naz-uh-REEN

Nazareth	NAZ-uh-reth
nazirite	NAZ-uh-rīt
Nazorean	naz-uh-REE-uhn
necessity	nuh-SES-uh-tee
Nehemiah	nee-uh-MĪ-uh
Ner	ner
nether	NETH-er
netherworld	NETH-er-werld
Nicanor	nih-KAY-ner; nī-KAY-ner
Nicodemus	nik-oh-DEE-muhs
Nicolaus	nik-oh-LAY-uhs
Nile	nīl
Nimshi	NIM-shee; NIM-shī
Nineveh	NIN-uh-vay; NIN-uh-vuh
Noah	NOH-ah
nonetheless	nuhn-thuh-LES
nought	nawt
nullify	NUL-uh-fī
numerous	NOO-mer-uhs; NYOO-mer-uhs
Nun	nuhn
nursling	NERS-ling
Obed	OH-bed
obliterate	uh-BLIT-uh-rayt
obstinate	OB-stih-nit

offense	oh-FENS
Olives	OL-ivz
Olivet	OL-ih-vet
Omega	oh-MAY-guh
Onesimus	oh-NES-ih-muhs
opportune	op-er-TOON; op-er-TYOON
oracle	OHR-uh-kuhl
oracular	oh-RAK-yuh-ler
ordinance	OHR-d*n-uhns
orgy	OHR-jee
ostracize	OS-truh-sīz
Pamphylia	pam-FIL-ee-uh
parable	PAYR-uh-b*l
Paraclete	PAYR-uh-kleet
Paradise	PAYR-uh-dīs
paralytic	payr-uh-LIT-ik
paralyzed	PAYR-uh-līzd
parapet	PAYR-uh-pit; PAYR-uh-pet
Parmenas	PAHR-muh-nuhs
Parthians	PAHR-thee-uhnz
partiality	pahr-shee-AL-uh-tee
paschal	PAS-kuhl
Pashhur	PAHSH-her; PASH-her
Passover	PAS-oh-ver
pasture	PAS-cher

Patmos	PAT-muhs; PAT-mahs
patriarchs	PAY-tree-ahrks
Paul	pawl
pendant	PEN-d*nt
Pentecost	PEN-tih-kost; PEN-tih-kawst
Perez	PAYR-ez
Perga	PER-guh
Pergamum	PER-guh-muhm
perish	PAYR-ish
perishable	PAYR-ish-uh-b*l
Perizzites	PAYR-ih-zīts
perpetual	per-PECH-oo-uhl
persecute	PER-suh-kyoot
persecution	per-suh-KYOO-shuhn
perseverance	per-suh-VEER-uhns
persevere	per-suh-VEER
Persia	PER-zhuh
persistence	per-SIS-t*ns
persistent	per-SIS-t*nt
perturbed	per-TERBD
perverse	per-VERS
pestilence	PES-tuh-luhns
Peter	PEE-ter
Phanuel	FAN-yoo-el; fuh-NYOO-uhl
Pharaoh	FAYR-oh

Pharisees	FAYR-uh-seez
Philadelphia	fil-uh-DEL-fee-uh
Philemon	fī-LEE-muhn
Philip	FIL-ip
Philippi	fih-LIP-ī
Philippians	fih-LIP-ee-uhnz
philosophy	fih-LAHS-uh-fee
Phrygia	FRIJ-ee-uh
phylacteries	fih-LAK-tuh-reez
Pilate	PĪ-luht
pilgrimage	PIL-gruh-mij
pinnacle	PIN-uh-k*l
Pisidia	pih-SID-ee-uh
pitiable	PIT-ee-uh-b*l
pivots	PIV-uhts
plague	playg
ploughshares	PLOW-shayrz
plentiful	PLEN-tee-fuhl
Pontius	PON-shuhs
Pontus	PON-tuhs
portent	POR-t*nt
portico	POR-tih-koh
posterity	pos-TAYR-ih-tee
praetorium	prih-TOHR-ee-uhm
precincts	PREE-singkts
prescribe	prih-SKRĪB
presentable	prih-ZEN-tuh-b*l

pretext	PREE-tekst
prey	pray
primacy	PRĪ-muh-see
principalities	prins-uh-PAL-uh-teez
proceed (verb)	proh-SEED
proceeds (noun)	PROH-seedz
Prochorus	PRAH-kuh-ruhs
procreation	proh-cree-AY-shuhn
procurator	PROK-yuh-ray-ter
prodigy	PROD-uh-jee
profanation	proh-fuh-NAY-shuhn
proficient	proh-FISH-uhnt
profitable	PROF-it-uh-b*l
profulgence	proh-FUHL-j*ns
progress (verb)	proh-GRES
prophecy	PROF-uh-see
prophesy	PROF-uh-sī
prophetic	pruh-FET-ik
propriety	pruh-PRĪ-uh-tee
proscribe	proh-SKRĪB
prosperity	pros-PAYR-uh-tee
prostitute	PROS-tuh-t<u>oo</u>t; PROS-tuh-ty<u>oo</u>t
prostrate	PROS-trayt
Proverbs	PRAH-verbz
Psalms	sawlmz; sahmz
purge	perj

purification	py<u>oo</u>r-ih-fih-KAY-shuhn
purifier	PY<u>OO</u>R-uh-fi
pustule	PUHS-ch<u>oo</u>l; PUHS-ty<u>oo</u>l
Put	p<u>oo</u>t
Qoheleth	koh-HEL-uhth
Quirinius	kwih-RIN-ee-uhs
Rabbi	RAB-ī
Rabboni	rab-OH-nee
Rabbouni	rab-<u>OO</u>-nee
Raga	RAH-guh
Rahab	RAY-hab
Ram	ram
ransomed	RAN-suhmd
ration	RASH-uhn; RAY-shuhn
ravine	ruh-VEEN
realization	ree-uh-luh-ZAY-shuhn
rebel (verb)	rih-BEL
rebuke	rih-BY<u>OO</u>K
recompense	REK-uhm-pens
reconcile	REK-uhn-sīl
reconciliation	rek-uhn-sil-ee-AY-shuhn
refuse (noun)	REF-y<u>oo</u>s
refuse (verb)	rih-FY<u>OO</u>Z
Rehoboam	ree-huh-BOH-uhm

reign	rayn
rein	rayn
rekindle	ree-KIN-d*l
reliable	rih-LĪ-uh-b*l
remembrance	rih-MEM-bruhns
remnant	REM-n*nt
remonstrate	rih-MON-strayt; REH-m*n-strayt
repentance	rih-PEN-t*ns
repentant	rih-PEN-t*nt
Rephidim	REH-fih-dim
reprimand	REP-ruh-mand
reproof	rih-PROOF
reprove	rih-PROOV
reputation	rep-yoo-TAY-shuhn
respectable	rih-SPEK-tuh-b*l
resplendent	rih-SPLEN-d*nt
resurrection	rez-uh-REK-shuhn
retinue	RET-*n-oo; RET-*n-yoo
retribution	reh-truh-BYOO-shuhn
Revelation	rev-uh-LAY-shuhn
revelry	REV-uhl-ree
revile	rih-VĪL
ridicule	RID-uh-kyool
righteous	RĪ-chuhs
rogue	rohg
Romans	ROH-muhnz

Rome	rohm
route	r<u>oo</u>t; rowt
Rufus	R<u>OO</u>-fuhs
ruddy	RUHD-ee
Ruth	r<u>oo</u>th
Sabbath	SAB-uhth
sacrificial	sak-ruh-FISH-uhl
Sadducees	SAD-y<u>oo</u>-seez
Salathiel	suh-LAY-thee-uhl
Salem	SAY-luhm
Salmon	SAL-muhn
Salome	suh-LOH-mee
salvation	sal-VAY-shuhn
Samaria	suh-MAYR-ee-uh
Samaritan	suh-MAYR-uh-tuhn
Samuel	SAM-y<u>oo</u>-uhl
sanctification	sangk-tuh-fih-KAY- shuhn
sanctify	SANGK-tih-fī
sanctuary	SANGK-ch<u>oo</u>-ayr-ee
Sanhedrin	san-HEE-druhn
sapphires	SAF-īrz
Sarah	SAYR-uh
Sarai	SAYR-ī
saraph	SAYR-uhf
Sardis	SAHR-dis
Satan	SAY-t*n

Saul	sawl
Savior	SAYV-yer
scepter	SEP-ter
sceptre	SEP-ter
scoff	skof; skawf
scorpion	SKOHR-pee-uhn
scourge	skerj
Scripture	SKRIP-cher
Scythian	SITH-ee-uhn
seah	SEE-ah
seclusion	sih-KLOO-zhuhn
seductive	sih-DUHK-tiv
semblance	SEM-bl*ns
sensuality	sen-shoo-AL-uh-tee
sentinel	SEN-tih-nuhl
seraphim	SAYR-uh-fim
seraphs	SAYR-uhfs
shamefacedly	SHAYM-fay-sid-lee
Shaphat	SHAY-fat
Sharon	SHAYR-uhn
Shealtiel	shee-AL-tee-uhl
Sheba	SHEE-buh
Shebna	SHEB-nah
Shechem	SHEK-uhm
shekel	SHEK-*l
Shelemiah	shel-uh-MĪ-uh

Sheol	SHAY-ohl; SHEE-ohl
Shephatiah	shef-uh-TĪ-uh
Shiloh	SHĪ-loh
Shinar	SHEE-nahr; SHĪ-nahr
Shunem	SHOO-nem
Sidon	SĪ-duhn
sieve	siv
Silas	SĪ-luhs
Siloam	sih-LOH-uhm
Silvanus	sil-VAY-nuhs
Simeon	SIM-ee-uhn
Simon	SĪ-muhn
Sinai	SĪ-nī
sinew	SIN-yoo
Sirach	SEER-ak
slaughter	SLAW-ter
Smyrna	SMER-nuh
Sodom	SOD-uhm
sojourn	SOH-jern
solemnity	suh-LEM-nuh-tee
solicitude	suh-LIS-uh-tood; suh-LIS-uh-tyood
Solomon	SOL-uh-muhn
Sosthenes	SOS-thuh-neez
sovereign	SOV-er-uhn; SOV-ruhn

sovereignty	SOV-er-uhn-tee; SOV-ruhn-tee
squander	SKWON-der
stature	STACH-er
statute	STACH-<u>oo</u>t
steadfast	STED-fast
stealth	stelth
Stephen	STEE-vuhn
steppe	step
steward	ST<u>OO</u>-erd; STY<u>OO</u>-erd
stupefied	ST<u>OO</u>-puh-fīd
sublime	suh-BLĪM
sumptuous	SUMP-ch<u>oo</u>-uhs
supplication	sup-lih-KAY-shuhn
surveillance	ser-VAY-l*ns
Susanna	s<u>oo</u>-ZAN-uh
swaddling	SWAHD-ling
sword	sohrd
sycamore	SIK-uh-mohr
Sychar	SĪK-ahr; SĪ-kahr
synagogue	SIN-uh-gog
Syria	SEER-ee-uh
tabernacle	TAB-er-nak-*l
Talitha cum	TAH-lee-thah K<u>OO</u>M
Talitha cumi	TAH-lee-thah K<u>OO</u>M
Talitha koum	TAH-lee-thah K<u>OO</u>M

Tamar	TAY-mahr
tarry	TAYR-ee
Tarshish	TAHR-shish
Tarsus	TAHR-suhs
temerity	tuh-MER-uh-tee
temperately	TEM-per-it-lee
tempest	TEM-pist
terebinth	TAYR-uh-binth
testify	TES-tuh-fī
testimony	TES-tuh-moh-nee
tetrarch	TET-rahrk
Thaddaeus	THAD-ee-uhs
Theophilus	thee-OF-uh-luhs
Thessalonians	thes-uh-LOH- nee-uhnz
Thomas	TOM-uhs
thongs	thawngz; thongz
thousandth	THOW-z*nth; THOW-z*ndth
threshold	THRESH-ohld; THRESH-hohld
Thyatira	thī-uh-TĪ-ruh
Tiberias	tī-BEER-ee-uhs
Tiberius	tī-BEER-ee-uhs
Timaeus	tim-AY-uhs; tim-EE-uhs
Timon	TĪ-muhn
Timothy	TIM-uh-thee

tithe	tith
Titus	TĪ-tuhs
tolerable	TOL-er-uh-b*l
tongues	tungs
tongs	tawngs; tongs
torrent	TOHR-*nt
torture	TOHR-cher
Trachonitis	trak-uh-NĪ-tis
transfigure	trans-FIG-yer
transgress	trans-GRES; tranz-GRES
transgression	trans-GRESH-uhn; tranz-GRESH-uhn
trepidation	trep-uh-DAY-shuhn
trespass	TRES-puhs; TRES-pas
tribunal	trī-BYOO-n*l; trih-BYOO-n*l
Tubal	TOO-bahl
Tyre	tir
Tyrian	TEER-ee-uhn
unanimously	yoo-NAN-uh-muhs-lee
unapproachable	uhn-uh-PROH-chuh-b*l
uncircumcision	uhn-ser-kuhm-SIH-zhuhn
unduly	uhn-DOO-lee; uhn-DYOO-lee

uninhabited	uhn-in-HAB-uh-tuhd
unleavened	uhn-LEV-uhnd
unmerciful	uhn-MER-sih-fuhl
unruly	uhn-R<u>OO</u>-lee
Ur	er; <u>oo</u>r
Uriah	y<u>oo</u>-RĪ-uh
utterance	UHT-er-*ns
Uzziah	uh-ZĪ-uh; yuh-ZĪ-uh
vehement	VEE-uh-m*nt
veil	vayl
vengeance	VEN-j*ns
vestibule	VES-tuh-by<u>oo</u>l
vexation	vek-SAY-shuhn
vindication	vin-dih-KAY-shuhn
vineyard	VIN-yerd
vintage	VIN-tij
visible	VIZ-uh-b*l
wadi	WAH-dee
wanton	WAHN-tuhn
weaned	weend
windings	WĪN-dingz
winnowing	WIN-oh-wing
Wisdom	WIZ-duhm
wrath	rath
wretch	retch
Yahweh	YAH-way

Yahweh-yireh	YAH-way-YEER-ay
Zacchaeus	zuh-KEE-uhs
Zadok	ZAD-uhk; ZAY-dok
Zarephath	ZAYR-uh-fath
zeal	zeel
Zealot	ZEL-uht
zealous	ZEL-uhs
Zebedee	ZEB-uh-dee
Zeboiim	zuh-BOY-im
Zebulun	ZEB-yoo-luhn
Zechariah	zek-uh-RĪ-uh
Zedekiah	zed-uh-KĪ-uh
Zephaniah	zef-uh-NĪ-uh
Zerah	ZEE-rah
Zerubbabel	zuh-ROOB-uh-b*l
Zion	ZĪ-ahn
Ziph	zif